Note: All activities in this book should be performed with adult supervision. Common sense and care are essential to the conduct of any and all activities, whether described in this book or not. Neither the author nor the publisher assumes any responsibility for any injuries or damages arising from any activities.

KINGFISHER
An imprint of Kingfisher Publications Plc
New Penderel House, 283-288 High Holborn, London WC1V 7HZ
www.kingfisherpub.com

First published by Kingfisher 2006
2 4 6 8 10 9 7 5 3 1

Text copyright © Kingfisher 2006
Illustrations copyright © Jan Lewis 2006
Created in association with the Complete Works
St Mary's Road, Royal Leamington Spa, Warwickshire, CV31 1JP

Edited by Jane Casey
Designed by Katy Walker

A CIP catalogue record for this book is available from the British Library.

ISBN-13: 978 0 7534 1383 8
ISBN-10: 0 7534 1383 3

Printed in China
1TR/0706/SNPEXL/MA(MA)/140MA/F

How to be a Pirate in 7 days or less

Illustrated by Jan Lewis
Written by Lesley Rees

KINGFISHER

AHOY THERE!

Welcome aboard the Jolly Roger, shipmates. I'm Captain Kid, a fearless pirate, and I'm looking for a new crew! I'm here to show you how to sail the seven seas in search of trouble and treasure. In seven days, if you follow my rules, you can become a pirate too.

Meet the crew!

Arrr!

Poopdeck is our noisy parrot.

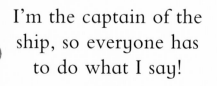

I'm the captain of the ship, so everyone has to do what I say!

This is my first mate, Barnacle Billy. He's not afraid of anything.

We sail the seas looking for ships to plunder and treasure to share.

Set sail with us, me hearties, and in one week we'll turn you into a fearless pirate with your very own cutlass. At the end of the week, you and your crewmates can celebrate with a pirate party. So shiver me timbers – it's time to come aboard!

BRAVE BUCCANEERS

Every wannabe pirate needs to think up a proper pirate name before starting their life of plunder and peril. Pirates choose names that tell other people something about them – I'm Captain Kid because I'm the youngest pirate captain around.

See if you can work out how these famous pirates got their names:

Blackbeard

Forkbeard

Little Jack

Bluetooth

Pegleg Pete

You'll need to choose a good name before you can call yourself a real pirate – try putting "Captain" in front of your real name.

PORTHOLE DOORPLATE

Make sure everyone knows your bedroom is the captain's cabin with this porthole doorplate!

WHAT YOU NEED:

- a pencil
- 1 large bowl
- 1 smaller bowl
- 2 pieces of card
- scissors
- glue
- a coin
- paintbrushes
- grey and black paint
- felt pens

1. Draw around the rim of the largest bowl on both pieces of card.
2. Carefully cut out both circles. You may need an adult to help you.

3. Take the smaller bowl and place it inside one of the circles. Draw around the rim.
4. Now cut out the centre of the circle to make a ring shape.
5. Cover the back of the ring in glue and stick it on top of the other card circle.
6. Draw around the coin at even spaces along the frame. These will look like the rivets that hold the porthole together.
7. Paint the whole frame with grey paint. Make the inside a lighter shade of grey and leave to dry.
8. In the centre, write your pirate name. You can trace the letters at the back of the book.

9. Paint on a skull and crossbones – you can use the template at the front of the book.

Now stick it on your cabin door!

Day 2

SHIVER ME TIMBERS

Now shipmates, if you're going to be a pirate, you have to look like one. Let's make a raid on Mum and Dad's wardrobe and we'll soon have you looking like a salty sea dog! Arr!

Roll an old pair of trousers up to the knee, or cut them so they look ragged. Ask permission first!

Add a baggy shirt or stripy T-shirt and tie a scarf around your waist.

Slip on a waistcoat or jacket, with a belt tied diagonally over your shoulder to hold your cutlass in place. Now tie a scarf around your head.

Some pirates went barefoot, but others wore long white socks. Wear them with black shoes and you'll look properly piratey!

Don't forget the finishing touches! Your pirate hat, eye patch and earring are in the pocket at the back of the book. Press out the earring and slide it onto your ear. Pop on your eye patch and pirate hat. Now you're a swashbuckling scoundrel!

CUT-THROAT CUTLASS

A pirate's best weapon is his cutlass. It has a long shiny blade, and it's razor-sharp. To be a proper pirate, you need to have a cutlass. Why not make one just like mine?

WHAT YOU NEED:

- thick card
- pencil
- scissors
- paintbrushes
- brown paint
- tin foil

1. Copy the cutlass shape from inside the front of the book onto a piece of card.
2. Carefully cut it out – you may need an adult to help you do this.
3. Paint the handle with brown paint.
4. Cover the blade with silver tin foil.

And that's it!

PERMISSION TO BOARD

Why do pirates sail the high seas looking for ships to raid? To capture the jewels and money they're carrying, shipmates! Check out the tools Billy and I use to help us find other ships.

I work out where to steer the ship with my compass. The earth is like a giant magnet – it makes the needle of my compass point north, so I always know the direction I'm sailing in.

Billy climbs up to the lookout post and uses his telescope to spot other ships.

When Billy spots an enemy ship, we speed towards it as fast as we can. When we've caught up with it, we attack with stinkbombs and cannon fire.

I spy treasure!

We capture everything we can – gold, silver, jewels, or even the ship!

"I SPY" TELESCOPE

Now make your very own telescope.

WHAT YOU NEED:

- ✖ two cardboard tubes
- ✖ tin foil
- ✖ scissors
- ✖ glue
- ✖ ruler (inside the front cover)
- ✖ paintbrush
- ✖ black paint

1. Make sure one tube fits inside the other.
2. Paint both tubes black and leave to dry.
3. Cut two strips of foil 5cm wide. Glue around each end of the larger tube.
4. Push the smaller tube inside the larger one. You can slide it in and out, just like a real telescope. Easy!

BEAUTIFUL BOOTY

We pirates take everything we can use when we capture a ship – even the ropes and sails – but we can't carry all of it around with us. We need to find a safe, secret place to keep our booty!

There's not much room on a pirate ship so we bury our treasure in chests instead!

TREASURE CHEST

This is how to make your own treasure chest.

WHAT YOU NEED:

- ✖ shoe box with lid
- ✖ thin card
- ✖ ruler (inside the front cover)
- ✖ pencil
- ✖ scisssors
- ✖ paints
- ✖ paper fasteners
- ✖ glue

1. Paint the box and lid with brown paint and leave to dry.
2. Cut two strips of thin card, 40cm long and 5cm wide.
3. Cut one end of each strip into a point.

4. Paint each strip grey and leave to dry.

5. Put the lid onto the box. Glue the strips to the back of the box and across the lid so the pointed ends hang over the front.

6. Lift the lid and fold back. This creases the card strip and makes a hinge.

7. Push the paper fasteners through the box in rows, like rivets. Fold back the metal strips to hold them in place.

8. Paint your initials on each end of the box. You can trace the letters at the back of the book.

Now you have your very own treasure chest. Why not fill it with chocolate gold coins and jelly "jewels"?

You have to hide your treasure chest in case someone else steals it.

Just be careful you don't forget where you buried it! X marks the spot.

Sometimes pirates weigh down their treasure chests with stones and hide them at the bottom of the sea. Barnacle Billy and I buried our treasure on a desert island.

Day 5

PIECES OF EIGHT!

When Barnacle Billy and I buried our treasure, I drew a map showing exactly where we'd hidden it, just in case we forgot.

I drew the shape of the island and all the important features, such as the palm trees. Then I drew the volcano near where we buried the treasure and marked the spot with an X.

TIME TO PARTY

It's time to make the invitations for your pirate party. Why not make each one look like a treasure map, just like mine?

WHAT YOU NEED:

- ☠ sheets of paper –
  one for each
  guest
- ☠ tea bag
- ☠ large bowl
- ☠ pencil
- ☠ felt pens
- ☠ wool or string

1. Put a tea bag in a large bowl and cover with hot water. You may need an adult to help you do this. Leave it to cool.
2. Draw a map of where you live on one side of each piece of paper in pencil.
3. Where your house should be, draw a pirate ship.

4. Mark out a pathway with a dotted line that leads up to your pirate ship/house and mark it with a large X.

5. Scrunch the paper into balls, to crease them, and dunk them in the bowl.

6. Unfold them carefully and lay them out flat to dry.

7. Tear the edges to make them look old.

8. On the blank side of the page, write out your invitation with felt pens. Write something like this:

> AHOY THERE, SHIPMATE!
> You are invited to a
> **Pirate Party!**
> on board
> **The Jolly Roger**
> (your address)
> **on**
> (date)
> **at**
> (time)
> **from**
> (your name)
> Please dress like a pirate
> (or walk the plank!)
> R.S.V.P.

9. Roll each invitation up and tie a piece of wool or string around it, so it looks like an old scroll.

And that's how easy it is to make your invitations. The hardest part is deciding who to invite!

Don't forget to invite me!

THE JOLLY ROGER

Pirate flags are flown to terrify other seafarers. The pictures on them warn sailors that fierce pirates are on board! Let's have a look at some pirate flags.

The most popular flag is the Jolly Roger. It's red – the colour of blood!

Pirates sometimes played sneaky tricks. They would fly a friendly fl[o] until they were close enough to atta[c]

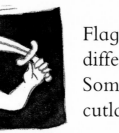

Flags feature different images. Some have cutlasses on them.

Some flags feature swords and hearts.

Some are decorated with scary skeletons.

FUN FLAGS

So how about making some flags of your own, shipmates? They'll look great at the party.

WHAT YOU NEED:

- sheets of paper
- pencil
- red paint
- black paint
- glue
- paintbrush
- drinking straws

1. Draw your design onto the paper. You can trace the skulls and crossbones from the front of the book.

2. Paint the background black or red, leaving your skull and crossbones white. Lay it out flat to dry.

3. Put a line of glue along one side of your flag. Place a drinking straw beside the glue and fold the glued edge over it.

4. Press down firmly and leave to dry. And that's it! Your very own Jolly Roger. Why not make a few more in different colours?

Day 6

GREAT GRUB

Being a pirate is hard work. We need plenty of yummy food to give us energy for climbing the rigging and leaping onto other ships. But pirate food is disgusting!

We sail around for months without stopping so most of our food is rotten. My dinner is always full of maggots!

Our biscuits, called "hardtack", are full of wriggling weevils.

We love fruit and vegetables, but we hardly ever get to eat them.

If pirates don't eat fresh fruit, they can get scurvy, a horrible disease.

Let's make some proper pirate grub for your pirate party!

———— SCURVY-BUSTING GROG ————

WHAT YOU NEED:

✖ lemonade
✖ orange juice
✖ ice cubes
✖ slices of orange and lemon

1. Empty a bottle of lemonade into a jug.
2. Add a carton of orange juice.
3. Stir to mix.
4. Add ice cubes and slices of orange and lemon.

Result – no scurvy!

HARDTACK

WHAT YOU NEED:

- ✖ digestive biscuits
- ✖ icing sugar
- ✖ cold water
- ✖ beetle-shaped jelly sweets

1. Place icing sugar in a bowl and add enough cold water to make a smooth paste.
2. Spread onto one side of a digestive biscuit.
3. Place the jelly sweets on top of the icing – they're the weevils!
4. Leave to set.
5. Gobble them up, especially the weevils!

TOPSAIL SANDWICHES

WHAT YOU NEED:

- ✖ sliced bread
- ✖ peanut butter
- ✖ jam
- ✖ cocktail sticks
- ✖ slices of melon

1. Spread peanut butter or jam on one side of the bread.
2. Cut into four triangle shapes.

3. Thread a cocktail stick through each triangle.
4. Stick the cocktail stick into the melon boat to form a sail.
5. Eat the sail first, then the boat!

DOUBLOONS, RATS' TAILS & PIECES OF EIGHT!

WHAT YOU NEED:

- ✖ gold and silver chocolate coins
- ✖ liquorice strings

Put the coins and liquorice on a plate and let your friends raid it!

CANNONBALLS

WHAT YOU NEED:

- ✖ marshmallows
- ✖ chocolate

1. Melt the chocolate in the microwave. Ask an adult to help you do this.
2. Dip marshmallows into the chocolate and leave to set.
3. Pile your cannonballs up on a plate and enjoy!

LET'S PARTY, ME HEARTY!

You've had a busy week learning how to be a proper pirate like Billy and me. You deserve a reward. So let's celebrate with a pirate party! Get all your crew together – it's time for some pirate party games.

— PASS THE CANNONBALL —

WHAT YOU NEED:

- ✖ gold chocolate coins (for the prize)
- ✖ sheets of black tissue paper
- ✖ music

1. Wrap the prize in lots of layers of tissue paper. Try to make the parcel look like a cannonball.
2. Sit your pirate crew in a circle.
3. Play some music and pass the cannonball around until the music stops.
4. When the music stops, the pirate holding the bomb gets to take off a layer of paper.
5. When the last layer of paper is removed, the cannonball has exploded! The pirate who's holding it gets the prize.

— PIN THE FLAG ON THE SHIP —

WHAT YOU NEED:

- ✖ pieces of paper
- ✖ bandana
- ✖ colouring pencils
- ✖ drawing pins

1. Draw a ship on a large piece of paper.
2. Get each of your pirate guests to draw a flag on a piece of paper and write their initials on it.
3. Tie the bandana around each pirate's eyes in turn and spin them around three times. They must try to pin their flag to the mast. The flag nearest to the mast wins.

SPIN THE BOTTLE OF GROG!

WHAT YOU NEED:

☠ a bottle   ☠ a list of tasks

1. Sit your pirate crew in a circle.
2. Place an empty bottle in the centre of the circle.
3. Take it in turns to spin the bottle. When it stops, whoever is sitting opposite the open end has to do a task (such as stand on one leg for a whole minute, or recite the alphabet backwards). If they get it right, they stay in; if they get it wrong, they're out! The winner is the last pirate left in.

CAPTURE THE FLAG

WHAT YOU NEED:

☠ a large area, outside or inside   ☠ 2 pirate flags

1. Divide your crew into two teams.
2. Mark out three areas – one for each team and a middle "neutral" space.
3. Each team gets five minutes to hide their flag somewhere in their area.
4. To win the game, you must capture the opposite team's flag and bring it back to your area. If you are caught in the opposition's area, you get taken to jail (a special place within their area).
5. You can be freed from jail if one of your team members taps you.

Got it!
We win!

Remember, no punching, kicking or gouging!

TERRIFIC TREASURE

Yo-ho-ho! Did you enjoy those games? Great!
Now it's time for the treasure hunt! First you'll need
to draw a big map, then add a few clues.

Hide your treasure in your house or garden. Mark the place on the map with a big "X", then work backwards to the start of the hunt, adding picture clues. Describe everyday objects around your home in a piratey way. Mark out the path with small crosses.

Get the idea, shipmates? Keep adding the clues until you get to the place you've buried your treasure. Make sure you bury enough treasure for all your crew to share, or you'll have a mutiny on your hands!

Desert island

Enemy ship

Sea

Coral reef

Now for some more fun and games, me hearties!

PIRATE TUG-OF-WAR!

WHAT YOU NEED:

☠ a long rope ☠ bandana

1. Divide your crew into two groups.
2. Tie the bandana in the middle of the rope.
3. Mark two lines on the ground.
4. Each group holds one end of the rope. The captain shouts, "Heave-ho, me hearties!" and both crews pull hard on the rope.
5. The first crew to pull the bandana over their line wins.

DRESSING-UP RACE

WHAT YOU NEED:

☠ a selection of pirate clothes

1. Spread the pirate clothes on the ground. Make sure that there is a whole outfit for everyone.
2. Mark a finish line a few metres beyond the last items of clothing.
3. When the captain shouts, "Go!" the pirates run to the clothes in front of them and dress up.
4. The winner is the first fully-dressed pirate to cross the finish line.

SAIL AWAY

So that's it! You are now a perfect pirate. Well done, shipmate. Barnacle Billy, Poopdeck and I can leave you to it, knowing you're ready to sail the high seas with your own crew.

But before we set sail, me hearties, we'll leave you with a few important rules you should remember.

1. PIRATES ALWAYS STICK TOGETHER.

Don't fight with your fellow pirates. They're your best mates and the ones you can rely on the most.

2. EAT LOTS OF FRUIT AND VEGETABLES!

That way you won't get the dreaded scurvy! Eating fresh fruit and vegetables is the only way to be a healthy pirate.

3. BEWARE THE WEEVILS.
Always check your hardtack!
Those pesky weevils get
everywhere.

One for you, one for me!

4. BE FAIR!
Pirates are tough on everyone
else, but fair with each other.
Share your booty with the others
on your ship, and they'll share theirs
with you – including chocolate
doubloons and pieces of eight.

And most importantly of all...

BE PROUD TO BE A PIRATE!

Arrr, shipmates, happy sailing!

ROUTE TO THE LOOT!

Play a pirate game!

WHAT YOU NEED:

- ✖ 2-6 players
- ✖ a die
- ✖ counters (from the pocket at the back)

1. Each player chooses a counter and throws the die. Whoever gets the highest score goes first.
2. Move forward the same number of squares as your score. If you throw a six, move forward six squares.
3. Follow the instructions on the squares – they can be good or bad! Climb up the masts and walk down the planks.
4. Take turns to throw the die and move until one of the players reaches the treasure and wins!

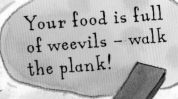

Your food is full of weevils – walk the plank!

You've agroun miss a t

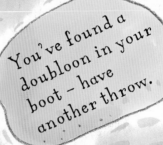

You've found a doubloon in your boot – have another throw.

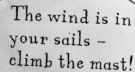

The wind is in your sails – climb the mast!

START

Trace over these letters to add the finishing touches to your doorplate, treasure chest and any other pirate project you like!

Aa Bb Cc
Dd Ee Ff
Gg Hh Ii Jj Kk
Ll Mm Nn Oo
Pp Qq Rr Ss Tt
Uu Vv Ww Xx
Yy Zz